MOTIVATE YOURSELF AND OTHERS

BULLET GUIDE

Steve Bavister and Amanda Vickers

About the authors

Amanda Vickers and Steve Bavister are directors of Speak First, a fast-growing global training and coaching consultancy that specializes in communication skills – including personal impact, managing the media, presentation skills, influencing, coaching and mentoring skills. They are experts in business communication and deliver training and coaching around the world for a wide range of organizations.

Before joining Speak First, Amanda worked for a global bank, both within the business and ultimately in a senior learning and development role, in which she successfully managed a team of 60 people. Steve worked at a senior level for an international media company, where he was responsible for a staff of 80.

Steve and Amanda have Honours degrees in Psychology and are Master Practitioners of Neuro Linguistic Programming (NLP), which gives them a rich understanding of what makes people tick. Together they have written a number of books, including *Essential NLP*, *Confident Coaching*, *Present with Impact and Confidence* and *Personal Impact*.

Contents

1. Theories of motivation — 1
2. The power of setting goals — 13
3. Motivating yourself — 25
4. Motivating yourself in practice — 37
5. Motivating others in practice — 49
6. Motivating others at work — 61
7. Motivating others at home — 73
8. Motivational killers – how to avoid demotivating — 85
9. Motivating people in difficult situations — 97
10. Becoming a great motivator — 109

Introduction

Have you ever wanted to do something and found it difficult to motivate yourself to do it? Do you look at other people and wonder how they manage to achieve so much and get things done? Or maybe you're adept at motivating yourself but have trouble getting other people – your kids, mother, father, spouse, colleagues or boss – to make things happen. If your answer to these questions is yes, you are not alone. Many people feel this way. The good news is that this Bullet Guide is packed full of tips, tools and techniques that you can apply straight away.

You will learn about many of the best-known theories of motivation, which means that you can apply what you discover to your own situation and make empowering changes in your life. Most of us have specific situations in which we want help with motivation, such as leading a healthier lifestyle, getting organized and gaining promotion.

You will also learn how setting goals motivates you to take action. Once you've established your goals, the next challenge is to make sure that they inspire you enough to see them through to completion. We all need a push from time to time – especially when our goals take time to achieve fruition.

Motivation is essential for success at work. If you're a manager or a leader, you need to create a motivational environment. You also need excellent interpersonal skills in order to motivate your colleagues and your boss. While motivating people is clearly important, it's even more important not to demotivate them. Taking time to pass on praise and appreciation reaps rich rewards at work.

For some people the biggest challenge lies closer to home – motivating children, spouse, parents, siblings, neighbours or friends.

Once you know what to do, it's relatively easy to motivate yourself and others in day-to-day situations. In some situations, though, you may find that what works with one person or situation doesn't work for another. That's when the information passed on here will help you to become much more creative in finding a way forward.

Great motivators never give up – they're creative in coming up with new ways of doing things, and they always believe that there's more for them to learn.

1 Theories of motivation

Introduction

What motivates people? Why **do they do** certain things and **not do** others? How can you **motivate people** – and **yourself**? These are questions that psychologists have puzzled over for years. Not surprisingly, they've come up with **plenty of theories**, and that's where we're going to start – by considering various **models of motivation**.

Summary

This chapter will help you to:

* understand popular theories of motivation
* recognize the practical value they bring
* appreciate the limitation of any one theory alone
* know that motivation is a complex field
* gain insight into what motivates you and others.

Motivation will almost always beat mere talent.

Norman Augustine

Carrot and stick

According to traditional thinking, people are motivated to **move towards pleasure** and **away from pain**. You can get them to do things by **rewarding them** with a carrot or by **beating them with a stick**.

You'll know from experience that there's some truth in this. People have a tendency to **move away from pain** and **move towards pleasure**. That's human nature. But what happens when you run out of carrots? Or put down your stick? **Motivation drops**.

Maslow's Hierarchy of Needs

Abraham Maslow developed one of the **most popular theories of motivation**, based around the idea that basic, **primal needs have to be met** before other, secondary needs become important.

It's only when people are fed and **feel safe** that relationships really matter to them – and after that **self-esteem** and **fulfilling their potential** become important.

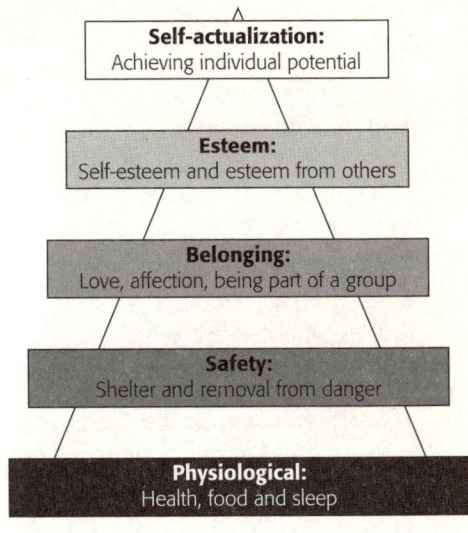

McGregor's Theory X and Theory Y

According to Douglas McGregor's theory, **many companies and managers** think of motivation as being either extrinsic (Theory X) or intrinsic (Theory Y). Characteristics of employees according to these theories are as follows:

Theory X (Extrinsic)	Theory Y (Intrinsic)
Lazy and passive	Energetic and active
Dislike work	Enjoy work
Have little ambition	Want to get on
Prefer to be led	Able to lead themselves
Resist change	Can be open to change
Need strong direction	Prefer autonomy
Have to be controlled	Are self-motivated

If Theory X is true, it's the role of **managers, parents** and **other agents outside the person** (extrinsic) to **provide motivation**, by threat or reward. If Theory Y is true, the person is **naturally motivated**, and all the external agents have to do is **nurture** this intrinsic motivation, and not demotivate the person.

Intrinsic vs extrinsic motivation

Recent research [see the book *Drive* by Daniel Pink (Canongate Books, 2010)] suggests that **only intrinsic motivation has lasting power**. If you're looking to motivate others, or yourself, you need to **harness it**.

External forces can **work for a while**, but only when the person really wants to do it, and is motivated towards a goal, will they put **sufficient energy and action** behind it.

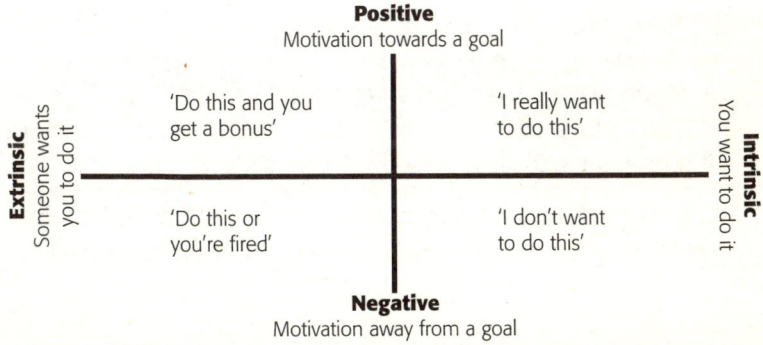

Herzberg's Hygiene Factors

Frederick Herzberg's contribution to motivational theory was that **certain factors are not actually motivational** – increasing them does not lead to increased motivation – but **their absence can lead to demotivation.**

Such **'hygiene' factors** cause frustration, unhappiness, dissatisfaction or even anger. Common hygiene factors include:

- **Working conditions** – e.g. too hot or cold, messy, noisy.
- **Job security** – e.g. is my position secure?
- **Status** – e.g. feeling that job title doesn't reflect contribution.
- **Relationships** – e.g. conflict and disagreement.
- **Pay and benefits** – e.g. not feeling sufficiently well remunerated.
- **Company issues** – e.g. policy, decisions, processes.

Ensuring that there are no problems in this area is **necessary but not sufficient** – you still need to find ways of **motivating yourself or others.**

Conditioning and reinforcement

Rats in a laboratory maze can be **conditioned** to, for example, press levers, by giving them food or electric shocks. The **stimulus gets paired with the response**. The same thing happens with people. When people are rewarded for doing certain things, they will continue doing them.

This means that we can **systematically shape** people's behaviour **by providing positive and/or negative reinforcement**. They will be motivated to avoid any kind of 'punishment' and motivated towards any kind of 'reward'.

Vroom's Expectancy Theory

Victor Vroom's Expectancy Theory says that people will **be motivated only** when they believe that their **efforts will be sufficient** to result in a reward that will satisfy an important need.

There are three elements to Expectancy Theory – expectancy, instrumentality and valence – each of which represents a belief.

Expectancy	Instrumentality	Valence
The employee's level of confidence regarding what he or she is capable of doing	The belief held by an employee that he or she will get what he or she has been promised	How strong the employee's desire is for internal and external rewards

Bullet Guide: Motivate Yourself and Others

McClelland's Three Needs Theory

In his **acquired-needs theory**, David McClelland proposes that people's **needs are acquired over time**, and their motivation is affected by **achievement, affiliation and power**.

McClelland's three needs

Achievement

Drive to excel, achieve and succeed

Avoid high- and low-risk situations

Need regular feedback to monitor progress

Prefer to work alone or with other high achievers

Affiliation

Desire for harmonious personal relationships

Need to feel accepted

Conform to the norms of the work group

Prefer work involving interaction with others

Power

Strong desire to direct people

Want to organize what others do

Seek personal and institutional power

Expect compliance and agreement from others

2 The power of setting goals

Introduction

When you **really, really want something**, you're motivated towards getting it. **Goals inspire action**. If you lack motivation, it could be because **your goals aren't compelling enough**. Or you don't have any. Your goal should be to **have lots of goals** – then you'll be motivated!

> **Goals provide the energy source that powers our lives. One of the best ways we can get the most from the energy we have is to focus it. That is what goals can do for us – concentrate our energy.**
>
> Denis Waitley

Summary

This chapter will help you to:

* understand why goals are essential to motivation
* set goals that will spur you into action
* make your goals as compelling as possible
* appreciate the importance of reviewing and renewing goals.

Goal setting – why it works as a motivator

Research in anthropology, psychology, evolutionary biology and many other disciplines **proves beyond doubt** that pretty much **all human behaviour is goal directed** – it's not random. **We have drives, instincts, needs and wants** – some of which operate outside of conscious awareness – that we seek to fulfil. **Knowing clearly what you're working towards**, by defining and specifying your goals, unlocks your motivation.

CASE STUDY

Michael was **unsure of what he wanted to do** with his life. He moved job every couple of years, with **little motivation** to study or progress. Then one day he sat down and **wrote out a list of goals**: get a degree, work in psychology, buy a house – and suddenly everything changed. **Once he knew what he wanted**, Michael had **no problem with his motivation**.

Coming up with motivating goals

Here are five ways of coming up with **goals that will motivate you**. Ask yourself:

1. What do I find most satisfying? **What do I most enjoy doing?**
2. How would I spend my time if earning a living and other practical concerns were not driving my behaviour?
3. What's **really important to me** at the deepest level?
4. Where would I like to be/how would I like to be/who would I like to be/what would I like to be doing in one year/three years/ten years?
5. How would I like to be remembered after I've gone? **What do I really want to have achieved** before I die?

Making goals SMART

The problem with many goals is that because they're vague they fail to motivate. **SMART will help you make your goals more specific.** Follow these steps and you'll feel more motivated:

- S – specific – make sure your goal is as specific as possible. You want to lose weight – but how much? You want to increase your salary – but to what level?
- M – measurable – how will you know you've achieved your goal? How will you be able to assess whether you're making progress towards it? It needs to be measurable.
- A – achievable – can it actually be achieved? Do you have the **necessary resources**?
- R – realistic – how motivated are you to go for goals that don't seem realistic? Exactly. Complete that project in two days? No way. **Make sure your goals are realistic.**
- T – time bound – You **must have a time frame**. If you don't, there's no sense of urgency, and you're not motivated to take action.

Breaking big goals down into smaller goals

How do you eat an elephant? **One bite at a time**! It's the same with goals.

While big goals can be **inspiring**, they can also be **daunting** – how will you ever achieve them? Breaking them down into **smaller sub-goals can help**, because you **feel a sense of accomplishment** when you reach them, which encourages you to continue.

Imagine you want to run a marathon. Here are some possible sub-goals that could keep you motivated:

1. run to the end of the road
2. run half a mile
3. run 5 kilometres
4. run 10 kilometres
5. run a half-marathon
6. run a marathon.

Achieving the **sub-goal** spurs you on to the next one. This is a simple technique you can use in just about any situation to make big and challenging goals more motivating.

NLP Well-formed Outcomes

From neuro linguistic programming (NLP) comes a model that **takes SMART to another level**: Well-formed Outcomes. The likelihood of achieving success is substantially increased when you meet a series of **rigorous conditions**:

1 **State the outcome in positive terms** Negative language places focus on what you don't want rather than what you do want.
2 **Ensure the outcome is within your control** Make sure you can get it yourself without help from others.
3 **Be as specific as possible** If your goal is woolly, you may not be motivated to work towards it.
4 **Use sensory-based evidence** What will you see, hear and feel when you achieve your goal?

5. **Consider the context** When, specifically, do you want it – and not want it.
6. **Identify resources** These can be internal such as skill, knowledge or self-belief or external such as money, equipment or helpful contacts.
7. **Make sure the outcome preserves the benefits** Is there a benefit from the current situation that might be lost if you achieve the outcome?
8. **Check that the outcome is ecologically sound** Would achieving the goal have any negative impact on other areas of your life?
9. **Define the first step** What is the first thing you need to do to move towards the outcome?

Making your goals compelling

Imagine if you could **go into the future** to the point at which **you have achieved your goal** and then look back to see what you did. **How motivating would that be?** Well you can – in your mind at least. And if you make the experience as vivid as possible – with all the sounds and feelings as well as the pictures – it becomes **so compelling** that you're naturally motivated to move towards it.

It's Wishcraft!

In her wonderful book *Wishcraft* (1979), Barbara Sher describes a fantastic process in which you *work backwards from your future goal* – one step at a time – until you reach now. The steps you need to take are obvious and clear, and all you have to do is take them. That's certainly motivating for most people!

Reviewing and renewing goals

A goal can **motivate you to take action** – but what happens once you've achieved it? It often loses its power. **Constantly review and renew your goals** to stay motivated. Here are five tips to keep you going:

1. **Write down your goals** – so you can keep track of them.
2. **Review your goals regularly** – at least once a month, and more often if possible.
3. Note when your motivation for a particular activity **starts to flag** and check whether the goal is sufficiently compelling.
4. If it's not, create a goal that's **bigger or stronger**.
5. Periodically think deeply and thoroughly about **what's really important to you**, so you make sure your goals, and motivation, are moving you in the right direction.

One way to keep momentum is to have constantly greater goals.

Michael Korda

3 Motivating yourself

Introduction

You've got clear goals, but **you're not achieving** them. Maybe you just can't be bothered. Perhaps you have made a start and **don't feel inclined** to finish. Or perhaps **your goals simply don't inspire you** enough to take action.

Whatever's going on, we all sometimes find ourselves with a need to motivate ourselves to **push through and achieve our goals**. Read on to **discover the secrets of success in motivating yourself**.

Summary

This chapter will help you to:

- understand what motivates you
- recognize the power of beliefs and values
- create a compelling personal vision or purpose
- work out what really drives you
- explore how feeling fit and healthy helps your motivation
- unleash the power of visualization and making things fun.

> **If you want to accomplish anything in life, you can't just sit back and hope it will happen. You've got to make it happen.**
>
> Chuck Norris

Know what works for you

Motivation is **all in the mind**. It's **an attitude**, a way of thinking about things. It's also about **putting action behind intent**. If you say you want to do something and you're not taking action, something needs to change.

What would it be like if you could **switch on your motivation at will**?

Well, you can. First, explore what's going on in your mind. What **stops you getting started**? What gets in the way of you continuing? **Change your thinking** and you **change your behaviour**. It's simply a matter of 'reprogramming' yourself!

Think about something you want to achieve. **Really focus on it.** Good intentions often fall by the wayside because what we want to achieve isn't **part of our usual routine**. Get started and **make it a daily habit.**

Creating empowering beliefs

Beliefs drive our behaviour. They're the **rules we live by**. Many people have **limiting beliefs** that **hold them back** from feeling motivated.

If you **believe you can** do something **you're likely to do it**. If you believe you can't, you won't — it's a **self-fulfilling prophecy**. But you can turn your limiting beliefs into empowering ones. Change the belief and **transform your motivation**.

Limiting belief	Empowering belief
I don't have enough willpower	I have lots of willpower
I'm not good at achieving my goals	If others can do it, so can I
I'll probably fail if I try	There's no failure, only feedback
I'll never succeed	I can succeed
I have to do things perfectly from the start	It's normal to make mistakes initially

Use your values as a compass

If you ask yourself **what's important to you** you're likely to come up with words or phrases such as success, recognition, humility, appreciation, love, having a home, getting promoted or making a difference in the world.

These are your values – what you consider important – and because they act like a compass that guides and drives your behaviour they are powerful motivating forces.

Stop and think for a moment about what's important to you – and then connect it with what you want to be motivated to do.

> **A man with money is no match against a man on a mission.**
>
> Doyle Brunson

Use purpose as a propulsion system

There's nothing more powerful than having a **clear purpose or mission** to **accomplish something**. **Clarify what you want** and you'll have a **propulsion system** that gives you the drive you need to attain it.

CASE STUDY

Charlotte was on a mission. **Her purpose in life was clear to her**. She wanted to help children get a good start in life by getting a good education. **Motivation was never an issue for her**. She trained as a teacher and **studied hard**. She realized that in many countries kids don't get the chance to learn, so she was motivated to raise money to **build and equip schools in Africa**. By the time she was 35 years old she had built her first school and was planning the next one.

Is it really what you want? Beware your 'shoulds'

Sometimes the reason we're not motivated to do something is because **we feel we should do it** – but at the unconscious level **we don't really want to do it**.

In any battle between the conscious and the unconscious mind, it's **the unconscious that usually wins**. So ask yourself – **do I really, really want to do this?** If you don't, **work out what's important to you** and do that instead.

Visualization leads to motivation

Visualization is **a powerful way of programming your brain** so you feel motivated to do what you want. Here's how to make it as effective as possible. **Imagine completing all the processes** that are involved in reaching your goal, and **what it will be like to have achieved it**.

Do

- ✓ Find somewhere quiet.
- ✓ **Relax fully** to engage your unconscious mind.
- ✓ See yourself as vividly as possible.
- ✓ Add a soundtrack to your movie.
- ✓ Run through the activity **from start to finish**.

Don't

- ✗ Allow interruptions (switch phones off).
- ✗ Worry if your visualization isn't totally crisp and clear.
- ✗ Keep thinking, 'Am I doing this right?'.
- ✗ Focus only on the end goal – include all stages.

Make it fun and enjoyable!

1. **Invent games** to make dull, boring and routine tasks fun.
2. **Reward yourself** for completing each project by spoiling yourself in some way.
3. Focus on **the part you like most** in the task and enjoy it to the full.
4. Treat each task as if it's **pure pleasure** to complete it. **Observe the difference** in how you feel.
5. Work alongside someone who loves doing the task – their enthusiasm will be contagious.
6. Turn a job into **a fun team activity** by getting others to compete in a race to get the job done.

> **In every job that must be done there is an element of fun. You find the fun, and snap! The job's a game.**
>
> Mary Poppins

Energize yourself to feel motivated

What sometimes **saps motivation** is **lack of energy**. And lack of energy often comes from lack of activity or eating stodgy food. **It's a vicious circle.** The less you do the less you want to do. Having a **healthy lifestyle** improves your motivation. When you're active, you **create a virtuous circle – the energy motivates you to get things done**.

CASE STUDY

Instead of taking the bus or driving into town, Sophie walks half a mile every day to work and back home again. She eats lots of **fruit, salad** and **fresh vegetables**. Her **healthy lifestyle gives her loads of energy** – and as a result her motivation for work and play remains high throughout the day.

4 Motivating yourself in practice

Introduction

Do you have a specific **situation in which you would like to motivate yourself** more effectively? Most of us do. This chapter is devoted to providing some of the **most common areas** where people want help with motivation, such as leading a healthier lifestyle, getting organized and gaining promotion. If your particular issue isn't covered, you'll probably find that **the ideas here can also be applied in your situation**.

Summary

This chapter will help you to motivate yourself to:

- get fit and live a healthy lifestyle
- learn a new skill and get qualified for a new job
- clear out your clutter and get organized
- complete the items on your 'To Do' list that have been on it for years.

> **Every day do something that will inch you closer to a better tomorrow.**
>
> Paul Parkin

Getting fit and eating well

Many people **sign up for a gym** at the beginning of January, **go a handful of times**, but **never step through the door** after the middle of February. 'Eating more healthily' is another popular New Year resolution. But, once again, people are often back on kebabs and pizza pretty soon.

One minute your motivation is sky high. Then it drops like a stone.

Been there, done that? Here are five great tips for keeping yourself motivated:

1 **Focus on the gain not the pain** Think about the benefit you'll get – such as looking good on the beach – not about the effort involved in getting there.
2 **Make your goals achievable** Don't be too ambitious or you'll soon fall short and your motivation will nose-dive. Can you really lose 20 pounds in one month?

3. **Track your progress** Are your jeans looser, do you have more energy? Measurable improvements increase motivation.
4. **Reward every small win** You said 'no' to ice cream and chose an apple instead. Well done! So give yourself a small reward (not a chocolate bar!) to reinforce the behaviour in the future.
5. **Amplify the downside of giving up** When you feel like giving up, imagine what life will be like in three months, six months, a year if you do. Tell yourself, 'I don't want that.'

Get skilled up

Playing the guitar? Speaking another language? Doing card tricks? Most of us have skills **we want to learn** – but **never get round to doing so**. What's that all about? Sometimes we really are **too busy** to progress beyond 'bonjour' or learn a few chords – which is **what we often tell ourselves**. But sometimes it's because we can't seem to **summon up enough motivation**.

That's often because **learning something new can be frustrating**. We go through four stages:

1. **Unconscious incompetence** – when we don't really know what's involved – we're in a state of relative ignorance.
2. **Conscious incompetence** – the awareness stage, when we do understand – this may be an exciting 'Ah ha!' period.
3. **Conscious competence** – when, if we focus really, really hard, we can do the skill moderately – but it takes a lot of effort.
4. **Unconscious competence**, which is mastery, when the skill becomes second nature – we can do it without really thinking.

The problem many people have is that it can **take an awful long time** to go from conscious competence to unconscious competence. This causes disenchantment and – if motivation isn't strong enough – giving up instead of crossing the finishing line.

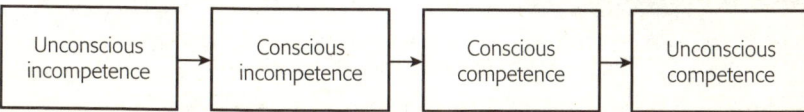

How to keep motivated when learning a new skill

- **Anticipate frustration** That will allow you to take it in your stride instead of considering it a setback.
- **Maintain momentum** When the going gets tough, or you get busy, make sure you still do a bit – if you stop you may not have the energy to get started again.
- **Break it down** If the task of learning the new skill feels enormous, break it down into 'bite-sized' chunks.
- **Do it with a friend** When you learn with someone else, you support each other when your motivation dips.

Ask yourself

Is it fear of failure and lack of confidence that's getting in the way of your motivation? If so, just accept that you will make mistakes along the way, but they will be learning opportunities and an essential part of your learning the new skill.

Getting motivated to study

Qualifications aren't essential for **success in life**, but they often help. The same is true of **personal development**. That can mean **studying hard**, **writing papers** and **revising for exams**. But with so many other – more interesting and enjoyable – ways of spending your time, **motivation can sometimes be lacking.**

Motivation tips for getting qualifications

* Keep in mind the goal and what **attaining the qualification** will mean for you.
* Focus on **aspects of the course you enjoy** – relish the process of learning them.
* Reward yourself in small ways for studying or revising for exams.
* When you feel like giving up, remind yourself of the benefits you'll gain.
* Tell yourself that you're the **kind of person** who **never gives up**.

Tackle your 'To Do' list

Have you got **things on your 'To Do' list** that feel like they've been there **since forever**? We all have. Items like this often remain undone because they either don't seem **important enough** to move up the list or are **too large** or **too dull** to tackle.

Now's the time to **get motivated to do them**! Here are two steps to nailing them once and for all:

1. **Start!** This is often the hard part. Once you've started, you'll be inclined to continue.
2. **Do a bit each day.** Develop a 'five minute habit'. Write just 150 words of your novel **every day**, and in a year you'll have 54,750 words – the length of many novels.

> **Motivation is what gets you started. Habit is what keeps you going.**
>
> Jim Ryun

The well of motivation

For many people motivation starts high and then dips. On larger projects it bumps along the bottom and then rises as the end comes into sight.

When you're going down into the well, know that it's natural. Look for ways of getting out as soon as possible, by thinking of the **consequences of not getting it done** or **how good it will feel when you have.** Keep going. As you get **closer to the finish line**, your motivation will naturally increase.

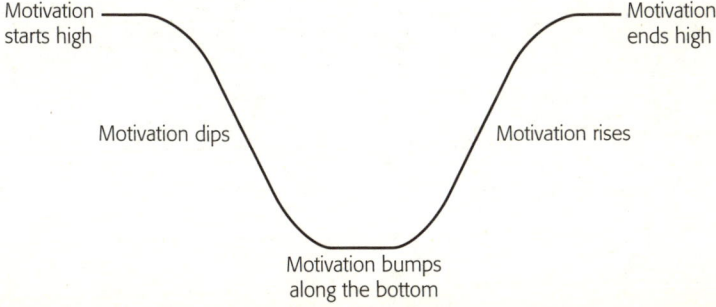

5 Motivating others in practice

Introduction

Motivation theory is one thing, but what about practice? We all know that people are motivated by different things. Some crave acceptance and recognition. For others it's achievement and winning. Some are motivated by challenge. Others pursue money and respond to incentives. Some have altruistic motives: to make a contribution or to build a better world. For others it's all about relationships, and getting along with other people. The list goes on and on.

Summary

This chapter will help you to:

- understand that people are motivated by different things
- harness the power of attaining and achieving
- motivate people by helping them avoid problems
- know how to motivate altruistic people
- understand how to motivate different personality styles.

> **Motivation is the art of getting people to do what you want them to do because they want to do it.**
>
> Dwight D. Eisenhower

Bigger and better

Some of us are **motivated by attaining** things. A bigger house, perhaps, in a better area of town. It could be a new car or the money to splash out on exotic holidays. For some it's more about status and the job title to go with it. Material possessions bring **a feel-good factor** and a **sense of worth** and value.

To motivate someone in this way you need to **connect with** what they're seeking. **Paint a picture in their mind** of what life will be like when they have achieved it. 'Complete this project well and you'll be able to afford that new car you're after with your bonus.'

It can **work just as well** on a smaller scale too. 'Your garden will be the best in the street once you've mown the lawn.'

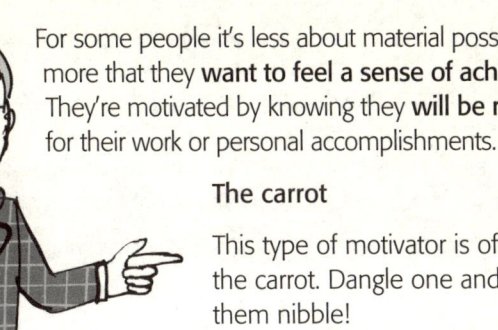

For some people it's less about material possessions and more that they **want to feel a sense of achievement**. They're motivated by knowing they **will be recognized** for their work or personal accomplishments.

The carrot

This type of motivator is often called the carrot. Dangle one and watch them nibble!

Fear of loss and negative consequences

A powerful motivation force for many people is to **avoid losing something.** Many advertisements use this motivator in phrases such as 'Sale ends tomorrow!' and 'Don't miss out!'. This has even more influence when they have something already and stand to lose it.

You can **harness this powerful force** by pointing out to people you want to motivate what they stand to **lose if they don't take action**.

Many of us are **motivated by avoiding negative consequences**. If you want to get someone to go shopping for food, for example, point out that they will have nothing nice to eat all weekend if they don't go.

Do

- ✔ Present people with **problems to be solved** and many will jump at the chance to fix them.
- ✔ **Explain the downside** if action isn't taken.

Don't

- ✘ **Focus purely on finding a solution** – this doesn't motivate everyone in every situation.
- ✘ Rely only on inspiring people with goals.

The stick

This type of motivator is commonly known as the stick. No-one likes a beating!

Making the world a better place

Some people are oriented more towards achieving things for others rather than themselves. It could be helping individuals or fighting for a cause.

While their **motives are altruistic** they may also get a feel-good factor from the satisfaction of having helped someone or having been part of supporting something much bigger such as a **desire to make the world a better place**.

CASE STUDY

Alice spends all her free time working with disadvantaged kids, and gets a kick out of **helping people** less fortunate than she is. **What drives her is a compelling vision** that one day everyone on the estate where she lives will have an equal chance to achieve something worthwhile. Because **she's so motivated** by the cause, she never finds it hard to help others, even after a long day at work.

What we have done for ourselves alone dies with us; what we have done for others and the world remains and is immortal.
Albert Pike

Motivating different personality styles

There are **four different types of personality style** and they're motivated in different ways. Identify your style and **adapt your approach** to motivate those with different styles from yours.

Task-focused, thinking, guarded

	Compliance	**D**ominance	
Slow Thorough Like detail Precise Reserved Indirect Co-operative	**S**teadiness	**I**nfluence	Fast Superficial Big picture High level Risk takers Direct Competitive

People-oriented, feeling, expressive

Bullet Guide: Motivate Yourself and Others

C styles are motivated by getting things right. They like things to be accurate and precise. Give them a problem to solve and they'll be content to work on it untill they find a solution	**D** styles are independent, impatient and are motivated by achieving goals and getting things done. They like to be in control so ask them what they would like to achieve
S styles are motivated by pleasing others and want everyone to get along. Stress how everyone can be involved and make sure there's a harmonious environment and they'll be happy	**I** styles love being around people and being the centre of attention. They're motivated by getting applause. Make sure you get them to work with others and make things sound exciting and compelling

6 Motivating others at work

Introduction

Motivation is fundamental to achieving success at work – and you **can't** motivate everyone the same way. The more you **understand what makes other people tick**, the better able you'll **be to get them to do what you want.**

If you're a manager or a leader, you absolutely must **create an environment where motivation thrives** – where people wake up in the morning and want to **do great work**. You can't do it all yourself. You also need **excellent interpersonal skills** in order to motivate your **colleagues** and your **boss.**

Summary

This chapter will help you to:

* create a motivational work environment
* become a motivational manager or leader
* pick up tips for motivating your colleagues
* know how to motivate a team.

> **Without a compelling cause,
> our employees are just putting in time.
> Their minds might be engaged,
> but their hearts are not.
> Meaning precedes motivation.**
>
> Lee J. Colan

Do this and you get that

Would it motivate you to get a job done on time or hit a target if you knew that **there was a bonus waiting** if you did? Of course. **Rewards and incentives work**. Successful managers and leaders often use schemes of this kind to **get people working harder or faster or more accurately**. If you're not doing something like this you're probably missing out on motivating people to push themselves to **do more**.

People are **always keen to have more cash** in their pocket, but it's **not just money that works**. Here are some other options:

Twelve powerful incentives and rewards

1. Pay rise
2. Bonus/commission
3. Improved benefits
4. Staff loan
5. Greater responsibility
6. More interesting work
7. Promotion
8. Better job title
9. Training/development
10. Flexible working
11. Social events
12. Leaving work early

CASE STUDY

Helen set up a team meeting to announce a new incentive scheme. Her aim was to motivate everyone to come up with ideas for improving customer service. She created a range of rewards people could choose from when they came up with an idea that was implemented. She carefully chose things that she knew would appeal to each individual.

> **You can motivate by fear. And you can motivate by reward. But both of these methods are only temporary. The only lasting method is self-motivation.**
>
> Homer Rice

Motivating your team

If you're a **manager or leader**, you need to **motivate your team**. Small things make a big difference. Like **listening to people's ideas, involving them** in projects and decisions and **showing appreciation** for what they do.

When people **feel that they are part of something exciting** that everyone in the team is focused on achieving, their motivation soars. Tasks take on a new sense of importance when people understand how **the part they are playing** is contributing to achieving the team goal.

Life at work, of course, isn't always plain sailing. **Going through tough times** together can be one of the best motivators of all – overcoming obstacles and challenging situations **helps the team bond**.

Do

- ✔ **Communicate clearly** what you expect of people and monitor it. What gets measured gets done!
- ✔ **Be open** to people doing things their way even if it's different from yours.
- ✔ **Listen to people's views** and incorporate them in your plans.
- ✔ **Know your people** and what motivates each person.
- ✔ Let them know they've done a great job.

Don't

- ✘ **Leave them to figure out the standards** you expect of them and fail to check their progress.
- ✘ **Micromanage** – giving them little scope for doing things their way.
- ✘ **Disregard their suggestions** and assume that your approach is the best.
- ✘ **Treat everyone as if they are the same** – adapt your approach for individual needs.
- ✘ Take what they do for granted.

Six essential techniques for being a motivational leader

1. **Inspire people** with a compelling vision and communicate it **with confidence and conviction**.
2. Be a **consistent role model** for others by doing what you ask others to do yourself.
3. **Be aware of how your mood is communicated** in your body language, voice tone and choice of words or phrases – if you're excited and energized, they will be.
4. **Let people know they are valued** by saying thanks for a good job done, take their views into account, and reward them with money, development and promotion.
5. **Demonstrate that you trust them** by empowering them to take on delegated tasks.
6. **Be there for them** – look after your team and they are more likely to look after you.

Top tips for motivating colleagues

- **Ask for their views** on projects, processes and everyday tasks.
- **Inspire them** to play their part by describing what it will be like to achieve a goal.
- **Explain the consequences** if they don't tackle problems or take action.
- **Thank them** for helping you out or for offering support.
- Let others know when a colleague has **done a good job**.
- Use 'we' rather than 'I' language when describing team achievements.
- Look out for opportunities to **raise their profiles** as well as yours.
- **Take a genuine interest** in your colleagues as people.

If you instil passion in people for their product or service, you don't have to tell them what to do about it because they'll do it for you.

Perween Warsi

Praise, recognition and appreciation

Do

- ✔ **Let people know** when they've done something well.
- ✔ Pass on praise immediately.
- ✔ **Tell them specifically** what's good so they can replicate it.
- ✔ Deliver it in a way that **works for the person** – some like public praise, others private.
- ✔ **Show appreciation** for the small things people do.

Don't

- ✘ Assume that they will know the good stuff and **only tell them what to improve**.
- ✘ **Say something general** such as 'Good job' or 'Well done'.
- ✘ Assume that everyone likes to receive recognition in the way that you do – **tailor it for each person**.
- ✘ **Be a miser** when it comes to praise – be generous with it.

Creating a motivational workplace

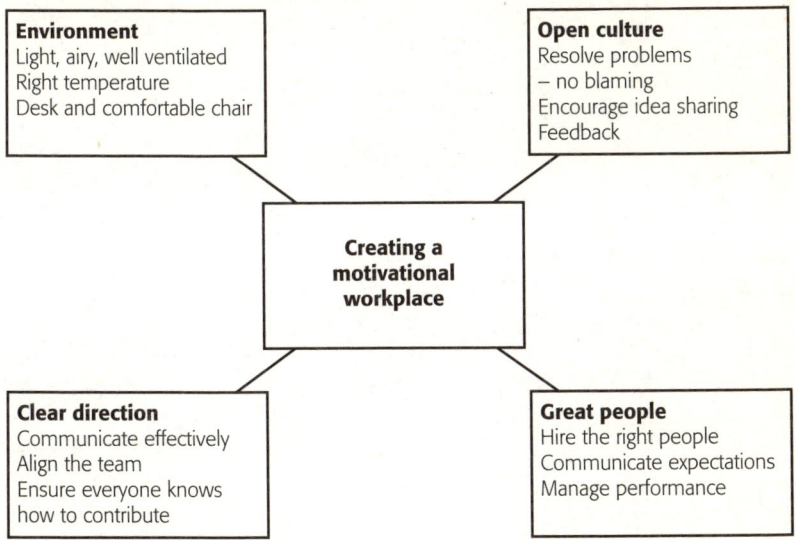

7 Motivating others at home

Introduction

How do you **motivate your children** to tidy up their bedrooms? Your spouse to **go away for a romantic weekend**? Your neighbour to be more considerate when parking his car?

Motivating people you don't know can sometimes be relatively easy, because there's **no existing relationship** to get in the way. But it's a whole **different ball game** when it comes to **family and friends**.

There was a time when we expected nothing of our children but obedience, as opposed to the present, when we expect everything from them but obedience.

Anatole Broyard

Summary

This chapter will help you to:

* understand why it's a challenge to motivate children
* understand the value of using stars and stickers
* encourage teenagers to do their homework
* recognize different ways of motivating youngsters
* get your partner to do more of what you want
* motivate your family to help you.

Motivating your children – why it's such a challenge

We all **want the best for our children**. And, with **the benefit of experience**, we think we know what's right for them. So we **try to motivate them** to do well, study hard, learn a musical instrument, make the right decisions, exercise enough and get a good job.

Are we successful? Sometimes. Sometimes not. **But resist reaching for the panic button.**

If you play your cards right you'll **be able to motivate them enough** to guide them into adulthood.

How to motivate your children

Do

- ✔ Appreciate that children are not small adults – their cognitive ability is not as advanced.
- ✔ Realize that children are more influenced by peer group pressure than they are by you.
- ✔ Try lots of different techniques on different occasions to see what works.

Don't

- ✘ Think that children will behave as you do – the way they think is different.
- ✘ Expect them to do what you tell them – it's entirely natural for them to rebel.
- ✘ Rely on just one or two approaches that will work only some of the time.

The power of the 'gold star'

Younger children are often **easier to motivate**, because they **don't spot the ploys** used to influence them – and they're not as cynical as some older children can be.

They respond well to incentives, so **giving them a 'gold star'** or a sticker when they do something you want works really well – especially if they get a **prize or a privilege** if they collect enough stars.

Sit on the 'naughty step' now!

If you've seen 'Supernanny' Jo Frost on TV, you'll know that the 'naughty step' is a physical location where **the child is placed when he or she has done wrong** – and then left to reflect on his or her misdemeanours.

It works very well with children up to the age of seven. Here's how to use it 'step-by-step':

1. **Stay calm and composed** – never get angry or upset.
2. **Specify the reason** – explain what he or she did wrong.
3. **State the duration** – how long on the step (and stick to it!).
4. **Be consistent** – always use the step when the child misbehaves.

From toddlers to tweenies

This is the time children are **most trainable**, so take advantage of it to help **build good habits**. Lecturing and punishing children often **alienates them** from parents, so aim to **build a solid relationship** that will hold you in good stead when they get older.

CASE STUDY

When 10-year-old Jack **didn't want to do his homework**, his mother sat down with him and asked him how he felt about it. She told him she'd love him unconditionally, no matter what he did, but that she wanted to **talk about the future** with him. Together they explored what might happen if he didn't do his homework and together came up with a schedule. Because **he played a part in creating it**, Jack was **motivated to follow it** most of the time.

The terrible, terrible teens

As soon as the **hormones start to kick in**, and **peer group pressure mounts**, motivating children as they enter their **teenage years** often becomes a nightmare. Try these techniques.

Do

- ✔ Treat them like adults.
- ✔ Only try to motivate them when it really matters.
- ✔ Build good habits when they're younger.
- ✔ Use incentives such as money and privileges.
- ✔ Practise what you preach.

Don't

- ✘ Speak to them as if they're children.
- ✘ Make a battle or issue out of every little thing.
- ✘ Wait until they're teens before getting involved.
- ✘ Think they 'should' just do what you want.
- ✘ Say one thing and do another.

Motivating your partner

Have you ever wanted to motivate your spouse or partner to mow the lawn, clean the house, get a job or something similar? Here's how …

Do

- ✔ Understand that they have their own way of thinking and feeling.
- ✔ Let them do it their way.
- ✔ Praise them when they do what you want – it will motivate them to do it again.

Don't

- ✘ Expect them to be like you, do things the way you do or fit into your mould.
- ✘ Insist they do it your way.
- ✘ Berate them when they make mistakes – it's a sure-fire way of demotivating them.

A happy home is one where each spouse grants the possibility that the other may be right, though neither believes it.

Don Fraser

Firing up your family

Because you know close family members, such as parents and siblings, so well you should **know which buttons to press** to get them fired up to do things.

One of the great things about close families is that **you can always go to them for help** and advice. Maybe you want to organize a 50th birthday party for Aunt Marie. By making your siblings or parents **feel part of things** you're more likely to motivate them to take part.

Most people **like to be given responsibility** for things as long as they're not overloaded. Trust them with tasks and they will **feel a sense of achievement** as well as involvement.

Families can sometimes be critical of each other, so make sure you avoid this or you'll end up demotivating them.

8 Motivational killers – how to avoid demotivating

Introduction

While motivating people is clearly important, it's **even more important not to demotivate them**. What's your motivation like when you're **frustrated or annoyed** with a person or a situation? Not very high. Even something as simple as **not being praised for a job well done** or not getting on with colleagues can **damage someone's morale**.

> **It's not my job to motivate players. They bring extraordinary motivation to our program. It's my job not to demotivate them.**
>
> Lou Holtz

Summary

This chapter will help you to:

- understand why demotivation can be damaging
- recognize ways in which demotivation occurs
- understand how pay and status affect motivation
- give feedback in a way that maintains motivation
- be aware of how people react when morale is low
- know how to avoid demotivating others.

Why demotivation can be worse than lack of motivation

Unmotivated. Demotivated. They're **not the same**, are they? When you're unmotivated you **lack motivation** – you don't feel like doing something. But when you're demotivated, you **do feel like doing** something, but you **can't summon up the motivation**.

What's going on? Well, it could be a number of things, some of which relate to your personal psychology, but more typically it's some outside influence that's demotivating you.

As a result, you lack energy and enthusiasm and don't have the get-up-and-go you need.

Bullet Guide: Motivate Yourself and Others

CASE STUDY

When Laura joined her company upon leaving university, she **was full of enthusiasm** and **highly motivated**. But now, after 15 months, **the shine has started to wear off**.

She was promised the opportunity to do **interesting, challenging work** – but much of it is routine and boring. She was told she had **bags of potential**, and would be given training and coaching, but so far she's only been on one half-day course.

Worst of all, her manager seems to **forget she's there** most of the time, and only speaks to her when **he's not happy** about something.

Not surprisingly, she's **planning to leave** as soon as she can find another job.

How to avoid demotivating others

If you do the following six things you're **likely to demotivate** people:

1. **Treat people unfairly** and deal with them dishonestly.
2. Criticize them excessively with **no balance** in your feedback.
3. **Fail to respect them** as individuals and the work they do.
4. Allow bullying, harassment and conflict in the workplace.
5. Put difficulties in their way or create unnecessary hassle.
6. Act as if **people are disposable** and unimportant.

Bullet Guide: Motivate Yourself and Others

Pay and status

Two of the **biggest demotivators** at work are pay and status. Here's what can **affect people's morale**, and **what to do about it**:

Demotivating issue	What to do about it
Pay: **below the level appropriate** for the role or level of responsibility	Pay: ensure that **pay scales are appropriate** to the role and level of responsibility
Status: job title doesn't reflect responsibility and contribution	Status: make sure that **people feel good** about their job title

CASE STUDY

Kim had **bags of motivation** until she discovered that the person at the next desk was **getting paid 20% more for doing exactly the same job** – so she decided just to do the minimum from that time on.

Giving feedback that's not demotivating

When giving feedback, do it the right way not the wrong way:

Right way	Wrong way
Focus on the behaviour	Make it about the person
Balance it with positives	Be totally negative
Make it specific, with examples	Make it general, with no examples
Be objective and factual	Be subjective and offer opinions

It ain't just what you say ...

The way you give feedback is **crucial to success** – and it's **not just the words that matter**. Equally important – sometimes even more so – is the quality of your voice. Don't:

* use an aggressive tone
* be any louder than necessary
* make your delivery **staccato**.

Feeling valued

We all want to **feel valued** … have a sense that **we matter** … know that **we're important**. That's why one of the easiest ways of demotivating someone is to act as if they're not there – as if they're invisible.

What to do

* Take time out to talk to people.
* Ask them **what's going on** in their life.
* Make them **feel important** in many small ways.

Job security

What's really important is job security. When people feel they **might lose their job**, or they may be moved to another position or department against their will, motivation typically goes through the floor.

What to do

Don't create **unnecessary stress** by making people **feel insecure** – unless there's a **real risk** of them losing their job. When people are worried, their motivation is **always compromised**.

Is that glass empty yet?

Emotions are contagious. The evidence from psychological studies and everyday life is overwhelming. So think about the **effect your state of mind can have on others**.

If you're a pessimistic, glass-half-empty kind of person, always looking at **what's wrong** or **why things can't or won't work**, you'll soon have those around you thinking and feeling the same way.

And if they're by nature optimistic, glass-half-full people, they won't be happy **swapping their rose-tinted glasses** for your grey-tinted ones. As a result, they're likely to feel down, and that will affect their motivation.

People generally prefer to be around others who are **positive and upbeat** – and, if you're not, you could **easily demotivate** them.

9 Motivating people in difficult situations

Introduction

With knowledge and practice it's **relatively easy** to motivate yourself and others in day-to-day situations. But **when the going gets tough** – because of either the situation or the person concerned – **you need to raise your game**. Your **existing strategies** may **no longer work**, and you'll have to **be more creative**.

> **Be miserable. Or motivate yourself. Whatever has to be done, it's always your choice.**
>
> Wayne Dyer

Summary

This chapter will help you to:

- motivate underperformers
- deal with sceptics and cynics
- encourage others to complete routine tasks
- know what to do when rewards aren't working
- implement strategies in difficult situations
- motivate others during a culture change
- know what to do when things appear hopeless and/or people feel helpless.

Motivating underperformers

People underperform for **different reasons**. Sometimes they don't have **the skills or knowledge** required. For others it's the **'will' that's missing**. They need to be motivated, using all the techniques in this book, if they're to give their best. The **Skill–Will Matrix** can help you understand what's going on.

	Low skill	High skill
High will	Guide	Delegate
Low will	Direct	Motivate

Don't lower your expectations to meet your performance. Raise your performance to meet your expectations. Expect the best of yourself, and then do what is necessary to make it a reality.

Ralph Marston

That's never going to work!

Sceptics and cynics can be **difficult to motivate**. They may **not buy into something** because they 'know' it won't work. They lack commitment because it **doesn't make sense** or it's not been thought through.

What can you do? Well, it's **not easy**, and in some cases **may be impossible**. You can only motivate them **if you can convince them**. Here's your best hope:

1. Allow them to **raise their concerns** and agree with anything you can.
2. Deal factually and unemotionally with **any misunderstandings** they have.
3. **Involve them** in finding a solution to resolve the problem they've raised.
4. Ask them to come up with a better alternative.

'I don't care'

People won't be motivated to do anything if it's not important to them – and the same will be true of you.

Maybe your partner would like you to be tidier around the house, but that's not really a big deal for you – you're happy for the place to feel 'lived in' rather than a show house.

Perhaps you'd like him or her to *do more chores* and *not watch so much TV* – but he or she *likes to 'chill'* at the end of the day. *The chores can wait* until another day.

How do you *motivate* each other? The only way is to *get the other person to care* about the issue, and the best way of doing that is to talk about how *you* feel.

Dull, dull, dull!

How motivated are you to do dull, routine, uninteresting tasks? Not very. And that's **true of most people**. Try these tips – for **you and for any staff you manage**:

* **Get over it!** Every job has a routine element – just accept the fact and knuckle down to the job.
* **Sandwich dull tasks in between more exciting ones** Do something dull to the point where your motivation is flagging, then switch to something more interesting for a while.
* **Distribute routine work** If you manage a team, make sure you don't have some people doing all the dull stuff. Share it around, or you're bound to have motivational problems.

If you find the whole of your job dull, consider doing something different – something that you are naturally motivated to do.

Reward wanted

Incentives work. Rewards motivate. But sometimes they **lose their power**. What then? How do you **keep morale up**? And how do you **manage your own motivation** when the reward no longer seems to be worth the effort?

You could **increase the size of the prize**, if that's an option, until it reaches a point where resistance is futile – but pretty soon its effectiveness as an incentive will drop again.

The solution is to find out **what naturally motivates the person** – his or her intrinsic motivation – and find some way of using that.

Bullet Guide: Motivate Yourself and Others

During a culture change

Many people welcome change, but some find it affects their motivation – especially if the changes are unwelcome and they had little involvement in the decision and have no control over what's happening. The model below, created by Elizabeth Kubler Ross, shows the stages people often go through when faced with a sudden change they're unhappy with.

If you have a team you're managing through a change, explaining the shape of the curve and the stages can help maintain motivation, because they know that eventually they'll reach acceptance and move on. The same can happen for you if you're affected by change.

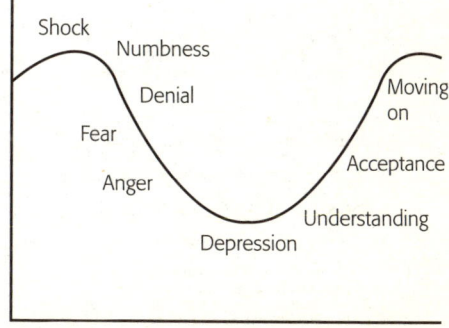

Motivation is low because of insecurity

Most companies go through troubled times. The economy rises and falls. Brand leaders lose their leading position. People get laid off. It can be **challenging to motivate yourself or others** when everyone is insecure about **the possibility of losing their job**, or **working twice as hard** for the same money.

Do

- ✔ Maintain a positive attitude.
- ✔ Aim to be as **effective** as possible.
- ✔ Focus on what's working well.
- ✔ Take action – which gives a feeling of being in control.

Don't

- ✘ **Worry and moan** – it won't help.
- ✘ Let things affect productivity.
- ✘ Dwell on **what's bad** about the situation.
- ✘ Drift along thinking it's **not possible to influence** events.

When the situation appears hopeless ...

... we feel that anything we do is futile and will make no difference to the end result. Hopelessness suggests a belief that we have no control over events. We feel we are a victim of circumstances over which we have no influence. The more unpredictable things appear to be, the more stressful it seems.

... and people feel helpless ...

... when they believe it's possible for others to achieve something but they're not capable of attaining it themselves. Once they realize that they are capable of doing it, they feel empowered again.

10 Becoming a great motivator

Introduction

The chances are that **you're already motivating people and yourself effectively** in some situations but **you're not world class**. You don't have a black belt yet! If you rate yourself at 6 out of 10 now, how do you get to 7 or 8? Applying **a few simple principles** that people who are excellent motivators follow will take you to the next level. Great motivators **never give up**, they're creative in coming up with **new ways of doing things** and they always **believe that there's more for them to learn**.

Summary

This chapter will help you to:

* make motivation important and focus on it
* vary the techniques you use leading to greater choice and more motivation
* check in on yourself and remedy any deficiencies
* constantly learn more about how to motivate yourself and others
* understand that motivation is a never-ending journey.

> **You were not born a winner, and you were not born a loser. You are what you make yourself be.**
>
> Lou Holtz

Making motivation important

In the non-stop dawn to dusk hurly-burly of twenty-first century life, it can be challenging to **maintain focus on motivation**. There's just so much to do! But when you **make motivation important**, you'll find it easier to achieve everything else.

Do

- ✔ Make *'**motivate yourself**' and '**motivate your team**'* number one and two on your 'To Do' list each day.
- ✔ Write your goals down and look at them every week.
- ✔ Put a sticker on your fridge or **create a reminder** on Outlook saying 'Motivate!'.

Don't

- ✘ Only think about motivation once a year when you review your goals or chat to your manager about your performance.
- ✘ Create goals and then forget about them.
- ✘ Get so absorbed in the day-to-day stuff that you don't reflect on your motivation and the impact you have on others.

Bullet Guide: Motivate Yourself and Others

Set your sights on becoming a world-class motivator

When you're **a world-class motivator** you have the **world at your feet**. But how do you become one? Easy: **you work at it** the same way you would anything else. You have to **learn the skills**, then **put them into practice.**

One step at a time, one day at a time, you get better and better at motivating yourself and others.

Ask yourself

What could I achieve if I was totally motivated to do what I want to do?

What could I get others to do if I could motivate them to the max?

Don't be a one-trick pony

Many people have a **limited toolkit** when it comes to motivating others or themselves – **just a couple of techniques** they come back to time and again, whether they work or not.

If you're a one-trick pony **you'll be ineffective** at motivating certain kinds of people and in certain kinds of situation.

A **one-size-fits-all approach** will take you only so far. You need to **expand the range of strategies** you have at your disposal.

If **what you're doing isn't working, try something different** – and keep trying until you find the key that opens the lock.

Never, never, never give up.
Winston Churchill

Where do I need to improve?

Those **on a mission** to become great motivators are **aware of their strengths and their weaknesses**. Are you? Do you know what you're good at when it comes to motivation, and where you're lacking?

Time to carry out a motivation audit! Once you've found out what's working and what isn't, all you have to do is figure **out how to fix it** – and then **do it**.

Motivation audit

Six tips for establishing your strengths and weaknesses:

1. Talk to **people you trust** – friends, colleagues, family – and insist that they give you honest feedback.
2. Ask them: 'In what ways am I good at motivating, and in what ways am I bad?'
3. **Push and probe** if they seem to be holding back – say, 'I really want/need to know'.
4. **Observe your own behaviour**: when are you effective at motivating and when are you not?
5. **Read other people** – gauge their reactions; are you sometimes demotivating them?
6. Notice when you can and can't motivate yourself – what's going on?

Feedback is the breakfast of champions.

Ken Blanchard

Three steps to getting where you want to be

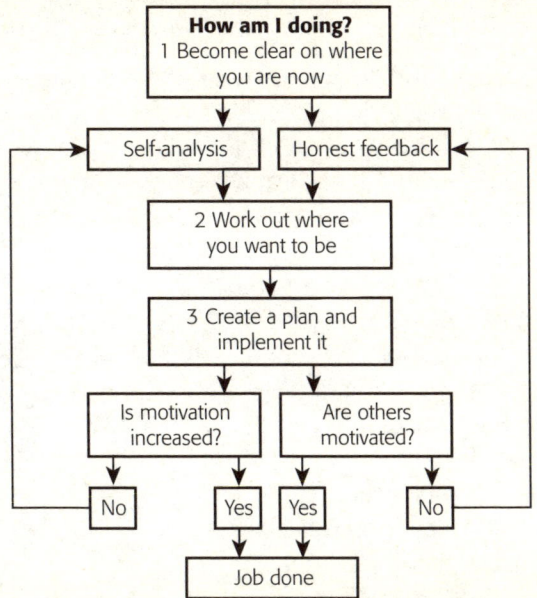

Getting better and better at motivating

Six ways to enhance your motivation knowledge and skills are:

1. **Read books and go online** There's a lot of material available from booksellers and via the Internet, much of it free of charge on blogs.
2. **Check out some videos** Go to sites such as YouTube and ted.com and you'll find video clips that will enhance your knowledge.
3. **Tune in to some audio** Top up your understanding on the move with podcasts and audio books from your mobile or laptop.
4. **Attend a seminar or workshop** There's no better way of improving your skills in this area.
5. **Talk to people who are really motivated** What's their secret? Ask them to share it with you.
6. **Read this book again (and again)** There's lots to digest and you won't take it all in at one sitting.

It's a never-ending journey!

Learning how to motivate yourself and others effectively is **a never-ending journey**. It's always **work in progress** – there's **always more to learn**.

Every day for the rest of your life you have **the opportunity to practise and develop** the **skills, attitudes and behaviours** that lead to being a world-class motivator.

The secret is to **make motivation a way of life,** not something you do once in a while. Eventually it will become part of **who you are** – a motivated person who is also good at motivating others.

So keep focusing on it. Keep improving. And keep motivated.

> **Motivation is like food for the brain. You cannot get enough in one sitting – it needs continual and regular top-ups.**
>
> Peter Davies